Christopher McNall is a barrister at 18 St John Street Chambers, Manchester where he specialises in disputes about tenanted and free-hold farms and land (and especially agricultural tenancies under the Agricultural Holdings Act 1986), taxation (especially of agricultural land), proprietary estoppel, and inheritance. He has appeared in many leading agricultural and tax cases in the Court of Appeal, the High Court, the Agricultural Lands Tribunal, and the First-tier Tribunal. He is Chairperson of the Agricultural Lands Tribunal for Wales, a Deputy District Judge, and a fee-paid Judge of the Tax and Property Chambers of the First-tier Tribunal. He was Consultant Editor for the 'Agricultural Holdings and Allotments' title in the 2018 edition of Halsbury's Laws of England and writes the 'View from the Bar' column for the Agricultural and Rural Affairs section of Practical Law. The views expressed in this book are entirely his personal views.

A Practical Guide to Agricultural Law and Tenancies

A Practical Guide to Agricultural Law and Tenancies

Christopher McNall
MA (Oxon) DPhil (Oxon) FALA
Barrister, 18 St John Street Chambers, Manchester

Law Brief Publishing

Published 2019 by Law Brief Publishing, an imprint of Law Brief Publishing Ltd
30 The Parks
Minehead
Somerset
TA24 8BT

www.lawbriefpublishing.com

Paperback: 978-1-912687-36-7

To my Mum and Dad

PREFACE

This book is an introduction for the non-specialist practitioner. Given its brevity, it cannot aim to be even remotely comprehensive, nor to be any substitute for specialist practitioners' works. However, and even though this book is only introductory, in reading it you are taking a worthwhile step in improving your knowledge of this interesting and challenging topic.

This book aims to be useful and value for money by guiding you round some of the main landmarks of agricultural law in England and Wales. Its approach is practical and not academic. Along the way, I shall point out some of the biggest pitfalls to avoid. All this, from beginning to end, should take no more than a couple of uninterrupted hours of your time.

If this book does its job, it will give you enough knowledge to be able to identify an agricultural law problem when you see one, and, having done so, to know that the problem may have to be dealt with using special tools, rather than by mixing and matching knowledge from other forms of commercial land-holding (such as business tenancies under the Landlord and Tenant Act 1954).

I gratefully acknowledge the friendship and support of Oliver Wilson, who sent me my very first set of instructions in an agricultural dispute, and his colleagues (past and present) at Nigel Davis Solicitors – Matthew Elias, Vito Berzanskis, Jacqui Mann, Louise Corbett, Joseph Mitchell, and especially Liz Power – for their combined knowledge and insight in cases too many to mention. The status of agricultural law as a distinct field of expertise owes much to Nigel Davis, Graham Smith and Eleanor Pinfold, who created and led the Agricultural Law Association's Fellowship programme, now in its tenth year. I also thank Geoff Whittaker and Mike Holland who have regularly published my articles in the Bulletin of the Agricultural Law Association. Finally, I have been lucky to have worked alongside, and learnt from, many skilled fellow practitioners. In this regard, special mention is due to David Kirwan at Kirwan's Solicitors, Tim Russ at Roythornes, and Kevin Kennedy, Heather Leach and Maddie Dunn at Burges Salmon.

This book aims to state the law of England and Wales as at 1 April 2019.

Christopher McNall
April 2019

CONTENTS

CHAPTER ONE
INTRODUCTION

Agriculture is important because most of the land in England and Wales (about 70%) is agricultural land. 'Agricultural law' is a slight misnomer. It is largely the law of agricultural landlord and tenant. This is because much agricultural land is tenanted. There are hundreds of thousands of tenanted farms – from massive moorland sprawls, to tiny arable patches – with everything in between. The average size is about 140 acres (140 football pitches).

This book will concentrate on two aspects of the law of agricultural landlord and tenant which are regularly encountered but sometimes imperfectly understood: the recovery of possession of agricultural holdings under the Agricultural Holdings 1986 Act ('**the 1986 Act**') and the making and opposition to succession applications to agricultural tenancies under the 1986 Act.

Agricultural tenancy disputes abound, fuelled by two important trends. One is that farmland is increasing in value: over the last 10 years, it has increased in value by more than gold. The other is that farming tenants are getting older and so the incidence of death and retirement is ever increasing. In 2013 about 2/3rds of agricultural tenants were 55 or older. A tenant's death or retirement is (at least potentially) a succession event for a 1986 Act tenancy and thereby gives rise to dispute and tactical manoeuvres.

Judicial resolution of many disputes does not lie in the court system, but instead lies (in England) with the Agricultural Lands and Drainage Division of the Property Chamber of the First-tier Tribunal and (in Wales) with the Agricultural Land Tribunal for Wales / Tribiwnlys Tir Amaethyddol yng Nghymru. In this text, I shall refer to these as 'the Tribunal'.

CHAPTER TWO
THE TWO TYPES OF AGRICULTURAL TENANCIES

There are two main Acts of Parliament which apply to tenanted agricultural land. The statutes are mutually exclusive. Any individual piece of tenanted land is held under the terms of one, or the other. It cannot be held under both.

The earliest is the Agricultural Holdings Act 1986 ('**the 1986 Act**'). Tenancies under the 1986 Act are often called 'AHTs' ('Agricultural Holding Tenancies') or '86 Act tenancies'.

The 1986 Act is a consolidating act, and replaces – albeit in largely identical terms – the Agricultural Holdings Act 1948 ('**the 1948 Act**'). As such, reported decisions about the meaning and effect of the 1948 Act can and often are applied to disputes about the same provision in the 1986 Act. Tenancies granted as early as 1948 (but which are now subject to the 1986 Act) still exist. 1986 Act tenancies are not only common but give rise to a host of challenging technical issues.

The later statute is the Agricultural Tenancies Act 1995 ('**the 1995 Act**'). Tenancies under the 1995 Act are often called 'FBTs' ('Farm Business Tenancies') or '95 Act tenancies'.

The 1986 Act is still in force. It was not repealed by the 1995 Act.

The 1986 Act and the 1995 Act are chalk and cheese. They could not really be more different in their content or operation.

The 1948 Act was part of the suite of social reforming legislation introduced by the post-War Labour government which also created the NHS and the State education system. The Act was designed to improve the fairly miserable lot of tenant farmers, and as a thanks for keeping the country fed in 1940. The 1948 Act, and now the 1986 Act, is definitely 'tenant friendly', not least in conferring what often effectively amounts to lifelong security of tenure. The 1948 Act, and the 1986 Act, are self-contained, very detailed, statutory 'Codes'. The answer to most questions about 1986 Act tenancies is to be found in the 1986 Act. There is some room, but not much, for the common law.

Tenancies under the 1995 Act are very different to 1986 Act tenancies. The 1995 Act, and FBTs created under it, are the product of libertarian ideas of freedom of contract. The 1995 Act largely leaves landlords and tenants to their own devices to strike whatever deal they want to, and the terms of their FBT embody that individual deal. Unlike the 1986 Act, the 1995 Act tenant never enjoys any security of tenure over and above the term granted. The 1995 Act is not really a detailed statutory code at all. It simply establishes some fairly basic ground rules. Beyond that, the parties are on their own.

This means that many problems which arise in relation to FBTs are best solved by looking to the tenancy agreement, and what it says. There are 'off-the-peg' standard form FBTs (for example, from the Royal Institute of Chartered Surveyors and the Country Landowners' Association). These are often very lengthy and detailed with sophisticated provisions for all sorts of contingencies.

However, because no tenancy agreement can ever deal with every possible eventuality, or be completely comprehensive, if you have an FBT problem and the answer is not in the tenancy agreement, then you are in the undesirable position of having to imply terms – if you can – by way of necessity or business efficacy. Going to court to imply a term into an FBT is not the most enticing prospect.

Which Act applies?

The best way of telling which Act applies is to look at the date on which the tenancy was first granted. If it was first granted on or after **1 September 1995** (the date on which the 1995 Act came into force) it cannot (except in exceptional circumstances – see below) be a tenancy under the 1986 Act.

1 September 1995. Remember the date!

If you want to stop reading here, you have already justified your outlay in the cost of this book.

If a tenancy was first granted on or after 2 September 1995, then you are most probably in 1995 Act territory and so probably do not need to trouble yourself with the intricacies of the 1986 Act.

Note the 'probablies'. There are some wrinkles. It is possible for a tenancy to be an AHT even if granted (NB, not first granted) after 1 September 1995. A good example of this would be a 1986 Act succession tenancy granted in (say) 2000.

1995 Act Tenancies / FBTs

Tenancies under the Agricultural Tenancies Act 1995 are Farm Business Tenancies ('FBT's) but are often known just as '95 Act' tenancies.

FBTs differ from 1986 Act tenancies in a number of very important ways. An FBT gives no security of tenure beyond that provided for in the tenancy agreement, and an FBT does not give succession rights.

In order to be an FBT, the tenancy must meet certain statutory conditions. These are (1) the 'Business Condition' and either (2) the 'Agriculture Condition' or (3) the 'Notice Condition'.

The 'Business Condition' is that all or part of the land is farmed for the purposes of a trade or business at the beginning of the tenancy, and some part remains so used at all times. The 1995 Act does not define 'farming'. Farming may or may not be the same as 'used for agriculture'.

The 'Agriculture Condition' is that, having regard to the terms of the tenancy, the use of the land, the nature or any commercial activities carried out on it, and any other relevant circumstances, the nature of the tenancy is wholly or primarily agricultural.

The 'Notice Condition' is that the parties have served on each other, at the commencement of the tenancy, written notices specifying that the tenancy shall remain an FBT even if the user of the land ceases, at some later date, to be primarily agricultural.

The Agricultural and Notice Conditions are designed to address different scenarios. The Agricultural Condition is suitable where, at the time the tenancy is granted, no substantial diversification from agricultural user is anticipated. Where the Notice Condition is met, the tenancy as granted remains an FBT, irrespective of whether the tenant changes the nature of his activity on the land from agriculture to something else. The Notice Condition therefore protects the landlord from an FBT turning into a business tenancy under the Landlord and Tenant Act 1954: that would be undesirable for a landlord since the 1954 Act would confer much greater security of tenure on the tenant than an FBT. For that very reason, in practice, the Notice Condition is almost universally complied with by prudent landlords.

Any tenancy of agricultural land first granted on or after 1st September 1995 which meets the statutory conditions for an FBT will be (and, if the Notice Condition is met, will remain) an FBT (and not a 1986 Act tenancy) unless it falls within one of the exceptions set out in section 4 of the 1995 Act.

The main exceptions are succession tenancies under the 1986 Act, and new tenancies granted over the whole or substantially the whole of land already comprised in a 1986 Act tenancy and containing a clear statement that the 1986 Act is to apply to them.

1995 Act Tenancies granted for a term of two years or less expire automatically, by effluxion of time: AHA 1995 section 5.

Tenancies for more than 2 years require service of a written notice (expiring on the term date) at least 12 months before the term date. There is no prescribed form of notice. If the FBT is granted as a fixed term of more than two years, then it can only be brought to an end by such a notice to quit. If no notice to quit is given, then the FBT will continue as a periodic tenancy (from year to year) until terminated by at least 12 months' notice expiring on an anniversary of the term date.

1986 Act tenancies

I have already drawn attention to 1 September 1995. Anything first granted before then is likely to be an AHT.

Here, there is another very important date. **12 July 1984.** Any tenancy first granted before **12 July 1984** will be a 1986 Act tenancy which will carry succession rights.

The right to succeed is not automatic. 'Succession rights' mean that an eligible and suitable successor can apply to succeed to the Tribunal on the death of retirement of the original tenant. This process can happen twice: from the original tenant to first successor; and from the first successor to the second successor. The 1986 Act sets out statutory tests to determine whether someone is 'eligible' and 'suitable'.

Bearing in mind that the original tenant themselves may well enjoy lifelong security of tenure, then extending that prospect not only to successor 1 but also, in due course, to successor 2 could potentially mean a tenancy lasting for well over a century. I frequently encounter tenancies granted in the 1950s where the tenancy is still in the hands of the original tenant.

So, the economic impact of a 1986 Act tenancy with succession rights can be dramatic. It is generally understood that the rent of an AHT carrying succession rights is less than the rent for an FBT, and that the presence of an AHT exerts a depressing effect on open market value. In financial terms, over three generations, and decades, this can be significant.

Any 1986 Act tenancy beginning between 12 July 1984 and 31 August 1995 will be governed by the 1986 Act, but with some watering down. These tenancies are secure for the original tenant, but generally do <u>not</u> carry any succession rights.

CHAPTER THREE AGRICULTURAL HOLDINGS ACT 1986

The statutory requirements

There are three statutory requirements for a 1986 Act tenancy.

Firstly, there has to be *'a contract of tenancy'*: section 1(1). In many cases this is easy to answer because the tenancy agreement is in writing (frequently using standard forms such as those provided by the Estates Gazette). But the 1986 Act does not require an AHT to be made by a deed, or even to be in writing. Many AHTs are annual tenancies, and as such (being tenancies for less than a term of three years) are exempt from the usual formality requirements for leases: LPA 1925 section 54(2).

Valid AHTs can be – and often are – created orally, just so long as the usual requirements for a binding contract are met: (i) an intention to create legal relations (family arrangements and 'gentlemen's agreements' may fail to satisfy this requirement); (ii) offer and matching acceptance (but remember – happening on or before 1 September 1995); and (iii) consideration.

Whether a tenancy is oral or in writing, the 1986 Act contains a mechanism for the implication of terms: see the discussion below about the 'model clauses' and section 7.

If there is no written agreement, then section 2 of the 1986 Act can sometimes engage. This section is a sort of 'statutory magic' which converts certain non-gratuitous licences and other informal arrangements which were in existence on 1 September 1995 into fully-fledged 1986 Act tenancies, '*where the circumstances are such that if [the occupant's] interest were a tenancy from year to year he would in respect of that land be the tenant of an agricultural holding*'. Interests of this nature are sometimes known as 'section 2 tenancies'. They are valid AHTs, but do not carry succession rights because they are deemed to have first come into existence on 1 September 1995.

For section 2 to operate, there still needs to be (i) an intention to create legal relations, (ii) exclusive occupation (meaning, at least, exclusive occupation for agricultural purposes, bearing in mind that fields, unlike rooms, do not have doors and windows which can be locked); and (iii) some consideration, although the requisite consideration need not be monetary, but can be something of value, such as keeping the land in good heart (Mitton v Farrow [1986] 2 EGLR 1) or agreeing to reseed after harvest (Davies v Davies [2002] EWCA Civ 1791). There are exceptions to section 2. For example, it does not convert grazing or mowing agreements 'during some specified period of the year' into agricultural tenancies: section 2(3).

The second requirement for an agricultural tenancy is that the land has to be *'let for use as agricultural land'*: section 1(2).

'*Agriculture*' includes:

'*horticulture, fruit growing, seed growing, dairy farming and livestock breeding and keeping, the use of land as grazing land, meadow land, osier land, market gardens and nursery grounds, and use of land for woodlands where that use is ancillary to the farming of land for other agricultural purposes'*: section 96(1)

This is not an exhaustive definition. For example, it does not include the growing of wheat, which is an extremely common agricultural activity and which is undoubtedly agricultural activity within the proper meaning and effect of the 1986 Act.

'*Livestock*' includes '*any creature kept for the production of food, wool, skins, or fur or for the purpose of its use in the farming of land or the carrying on in relation to land of any agricultural activity'*.

The courts have interpreted this as ruling out, from being AHTs, instances where the agricultural activity consists of things such as pheasant rearing for sport and the keeping of horses (unless they are being kept to be eaten or to draw the plough, which would qualify the horse as 'livestock'). Whether equestrian activity is a qualifying activity for an AHT can still be a grey area: seek specialist advice.

The third statutory requirement is that the land used for agriculture must be *'so used for the purposes of a trade or business'*: section 1(4). Whether activity is a trade or business for this purpose can be a matter of fact and degree, especially when the business activity is quite modest (for example, the use of land to produce and sell a grass crop for a few hundred pounds) and/or is not conducted on conventional business principles (for example, where it is more akin to a hobby).

If there is agricultural use of the land, and the land is being used for the purposes of a trade or business, then that trade or business does not itself have to be an *agricultural* trade or business. For example, land used for grazing horses (an agricultural use) where that is for the purposes of a livery stables (a trade or business, but not an agricultural trade or business, because horses are not livestock) is nonetheless capable of being an AHA tenancy: Rutherford v Maurer [1962] 1 QB 16

The 'Model Clauses': section 7

Section 7 of the 1986 Act incorporates the so-called 'model clauses' into all AHTs, whether written or oral. The 'model clauses' concern the maintenance, repair and insurance of fixed equipment. Fixed equipment includes any building or structure affixed to the land, and any works on, in, over or under land.

The model clauses are incorporated '*except insofar as they would impose on one of the parties to an agreement in writing a liability which under the agreement is imposed on the other*'. This means that the liabilities contemplated by the model clauses will apply unless the parties have agreed something different.

The full text of the model clauses is to be found in The Agriculture (Model Clauses for Fixed Equipment) (England) Regulations 2015 (for England only) and the Schedule to The Agriculture (Maintenance, Repair, and Insurance of Fixed Equipment) Regulations 1973 (for Wales only).

The 2015 and 1973 Regulations are both extremely detailed codes which put liabilities for maintaining and repairing a whole range of fixed equipment on either the landlord or the tenant. So, if the agreement lacks detail, and you want to know who (for example) has to pay to fix the smoke detector system in the milking parlour, the Regulations should provide the answer.

The existence of separate Regulations for England, and Wales, reflects the fact that agricultural matters are devolved to the Welsh Government, and the Welsh Government and not Westminster has legislative competence. This is why the Tribunal in Wales (The Agricultural Land Tribunal for Wales) is not the same as the Tribunal in England (The Agricultural Lands and Drainage Division of the Property Chamber of the First-tier Tribunal).

Although the 1986 Act is the same and applies equally in England and Wales, the procedural rules which govern the work of the Tribunal in England (The Tribunal Procedure (First-tier Tribunal) (Property Chamber) Rules 2013: SI 2013/1169) are not the same as those in Wales (The Agricultural Lands Tribunal (Rules) Order 2007: SI 2007/3105). Use the right rules.

Schedule 1: Matters for which provision should be made

In addition to section 7, Schedule 1 of the 1986 Act sets out a list of nine '*Matters for which provision is to be made in written tenancy agreements*'.

Schedule 1 applies to all tenancy agreements, whether written or oral. Some of these nine matters are obvious, such as 'the term or terms for which the holding or different parts of it is or are agreed to be let' and 'the rent reserved and the dates on which it is payable'.

The most important item on the list regularly encountered in practice is Paragraph 9: 'a covenant by the tenant not to assign, sub-let or part with possession of the holding or any part of it without the landlord's consent in writing'.

If the tenancy agreement – whether written or oral – fails to make provision for one or more of the matters in Schedule 1, and if the landlord and tenant cannot agree what provision should be made, then section 6 of the 1986 Act gives a mechanism to refer that matter to arbitration. So, Schedule 1 (unlike the Model Clauses) does not actually give an answer to *what* the clause should be – it just gives the mechanism for the arbitrator to decide what the clause should be.

Assignment of a 1986 Act tenancy

Even though a 1986 Act tenancy is capable of conferring, in reality, what can amount to lifelong security of tenure on the tenant, this is not absolute. In relation to pre-1984 AHTs, the landlord may resist any succession application when the tenant dies or retires. Post-1984 AHTs do not carry succession rights at all. The obvious way for the tenant to try to sidestep either of these difficulties is to assign. Assignment by a natural person (who will eventually die) to a legal person such as a company (which, as long as it remains on the Register, may live for ever) is one way of trying to keep the tenancy alive. Assignments by natural persons to limited companies are frequently encountered, but it has to be borne in mind that, if the assignee company is to have the benefit of a 1986 Act tenancy, then it needs itself to continue to satisfy the statutory conditions, including occupying the land itself for the purposes of a trade or business. 'Dormant' or non-trading companies may fail to satisfy section 1(4) of the 1986 Act, thereby losing the protection of the 1986 Act.

Most written tenancy agreements contain an anti-assignment covenant. The covenant often implied into commercial leases (that is, leases under the Landlord and Tenant Act 1954) that the landlord cannot unreasonably withhold consent to assignment is not implied into tenancies of agricultural holdings. As such, assignment without consent in breach of an express anti-assignment covenant is a dangerous step to take. It risks being treated as an irremediable breach of the lease, thereby potentially bringing the tenancy to an end.

Where the tenancy (whether oral or in writing) is silent as to whether the tenant can assign, then there is a possibility of assignment.

Here, the 1986 Act – as a detailed self-contained statutory code – gives the answer. Where the agreement fails to make any provision for the matter in Schedule 1 Paragraph 9, namely 'a covenant by the tenant not to assign, sub-let or part with possession of the holding or any part of it without the landlord's consent in writing' then either the landlord or the tenant can request (in writing) that the other enter into a written agreement '*embodying all the terms of the tenancy and containing provision for all of the said matters*', and, in the absence of such agreement, referring the terms of the tenancy to arbitration or third-party determination.

A notice of this kind is given under section 6 of the 1986 Act, and is often referred to as a 'section 6 notice'. Such a notice has the very important practical side-effect of preventing the tenant from assigning, sub-letting or parting with possession, of the whole or any part, without the landlord's consent in writing, '*during the period while the determination of the terms of the tenancy is pending*': section 6(5). Any such transaction is void. A sensible landlord who faces an occupant who may be a 1986 Act tenant where the tenancy is oral, or is in writing but without any anti-assignment clause, should give urgent consideration to the giving of a section 6 notice so as to prevent assignment to a legal person.

There is an unresolved legal question whether section 6 notices expire automatically through effluxion of time. This has not yet been decided, and opinion is divided. Some landlords periodically issue new section 6 notices, all without prejudice to the force, meaning, effect, and validity of any previous section 6 notices.

Any arbitration as to the matters under Schedule 1 (as indeed, all arbitrations conducted in relation to the 1986 Act) is conducted by a surveyor, appointed by the President of RICS, under the terms of the Arbitration Act 1996. But the arbitrator cannot rewrite the tenancy agreement ad lib. Her power is limited to specifying the existing terms of the tenancy, and making provision for the Schedule 1 matters only where it is 'reasonable and just' to do so.

In contrast, the procedure under which a 'Third Party Determination' is to be conducted is not subject to the 1996 Arbitration Act. It seems that the parties are free to agree any procedure they want.

Recovering possession of a 1986 Act tenancy: Types of Notices to Quit

1986 Act tenancies do not expire by effluxion of time. Even death does not bring them to an end, since the benefit of the tenancy becomes vested in the tenant's personal representatives.

A key feature of 1986 Act tenancies is that the tenant's security of tenure is achieved by the imposition of restrictions upon landlords' notices to quit. The recovery of possession can be complex, difficult, and time-consuming. It is full of traps for the unwary.

The recovery of possession under the 1986 Act is mainly a 'notice based' system. This means that even when the tenant is in clear breach of a statutory or contractual obligation (for instance, the obligation to pay rent as and when due) that breach, in and of itself, is not sufficient to allow the landlord to recover possession. The landlord must, in most instances, give a notice. Under the 1986 Act, it is the giving of the right notice at the right time in the right way which entitles the landlord to recover possession – and not the underlying breach itself.

There are two main kinds of notice to quit AHTs, and they are governed by different rules.

The first is a 'general' notice to quit. A general notice does not need to give any reason (although it may) but it must be valid at common law (i.e., it must be sufficiently clear, unambiguous and precise: see Mannai Investment v Eagle Star [1995] 1 WLR 1508). Usually (but not always), at least 12-months' notice (expiring on a term date) is required, even if the tenancy agreement says that less than 12-months notice is needed: section 25(1).

The second kind of notice to quit is a 'Special Case' notice. That is a notice which seeks to rely on one of the 'Special Cases' set out in Schedule 3 of the 1986 Act. If a Special Case notice is to be given, it is particularly important to pay close attention to the wording of the Special Case and to get the notice right.

There is no restriction on the type or number of notices to quit that a landlord can give at one time. A landlord can give a general notice to quit alongside one (or more) Special Case notices. The giving of a Special Case notice under one case does not preclude the giving of a Special Case notice under another case. Notices are usually given expressly without prejudice to the force, validity, meaning and effect of any other notices. 1986 Act notices can also be given expressly without prejudice to the contention that no 1986 Act tenancy in fact exists (for example, if it is considered that the tenancy has already come to an end for some reason, or if the evidence supporting the existence of a 1986 Act tenancy is thin, or non-existent).

Bringing and challenging a 'general' Notice to Quit

A valid Notice to Quit ends the tenancy.

However, section 26(1) of the 1986 Act gives the tenant a safeguard. Where a general notice to quit is given and "*not later than one month from the giving of the notice to quit the tenant serves on the landlord a counter-notice in writing requiring that this subsection shall not apply to the notice to quit"* then (subject to s 26(2)) the notice to quit shall not have effect unless, on an application by the landlord, the Tribunal consents to its operation.

Speed is of the essence! In responding to a general notice to quit, the tenant's counter-notice must be served within one month. This is a rigid and inflexible time limit. The Tribunal does not have any power or discretion to extend the time limit for the tenant's counter-notice. If the tenant fails to give a counter-notice in time, then the general Notice to Quit becomes 'incontestable', and (unless it is invalid for some reason at common law, e.g. for vagueness, or because it expires on the wrong day) it will bring the tenancy to an end.

There is no prescribed form which the tenant's counter-notice should take. It can be as simple as a letter, but it must make clear that the tenant proposes to rely on section 26 and wishes to refer the general Notice to Quit to the Tribunal.

If the tenant does this, in time, then the general notice to quit is not effective unless and until the landlord applies to the Tribunal (himself, within a specified timeframe, but which can be extended by the Tribunal) and the Tribunal consents to its operation. If the landlord does not make such an application, then the notice to quit loses its effect.

But the landlord then faces two further hurdles. The first is that the Tribunal will only give consent if the landlord satisfies it that one or more of the six statutory grounds (set out in section 27) for the recovery of possession applies. These are (a) 'good husbandry';

(b) 'sound management of the estate'; (c) 'agricultural research or education, or for the purposes of the enactments relating to smallholdings'; (d) 'a purpose desirable for the enactments relating to allotments'; (e) 'greater hardship would be caused by withholding than by giving consent'; and (f) 'the landlord proposes to terminate the tenancy for a non-agricultural purpose'.

None of these grounds are entirely straightforward for the landlord to establish.

Even if the landlord does succeed in establishing the ground, the Tribunal still has a discretion as to whether it gives its consent because the Tribunal must (not 'may') withhold consent if satisfied that 'in all the circumstances it appears to them that a fair and reasonable landlord would not insist on possession'. That is obviously a fact-sensitive decision. The 1986 Act does not give any further guidance, and nor do the reported cases.

It is technically possible (although in reality unlikely) that a Tribunal could consider that greater hardship would be caused to the landlord by withholding consent than to the tenant by giving consent but that nonetheless a fair and reasonable landlord would still not insist on possession, meaning that the Tribunal would not consent to the operation of the general Notice to Quit.

Bringing and challenging a 'Special Case' Notice to Quit

Case A: Smallholdings

There are five requirements to a successful Case A Notice to Quit, which must all be satisfied:

i. A smallholding under Agriculture Act 1970; and

ii. Let after 12th September 1984; and

iii. The Tenant is over 65; and

iv. Suitable alternative living accommodation is available; and

v. The tenancy agreement contains a statement that Case A shall apply.

Case A is infrequently met since it is available only to local authority landlords who have smallholding estates ('county farms estates') within the meaning of the Agriculture Act 1970. These smallholdings were intended as 'starter farms', but some smallholders have not moved on to larger farms and remain in possession decades later.

The tenant's challenge to a Case A Notice to Quit begins with a 'Demand for Arbitration'. There is no prescribed form for this, but it must be in writing and must make clear that the tenant disputes the validity of the reason(s) given in the Notice to Quit, and demands arbitration. This demand must be given within one month of service of the notice to quit. If that is not done, then the Notice to Quit cannot be challenged at arbitration.

If arbitration is demanded, then the notice must be referred to arbitration. This is also subject to a time limit.

This is an arbitration before a surveyor appointed as an arbitrator by the President of RICS under its Dispute Resolution Service. The provisions of the Arbitration Act 1996 apply to the arbitration. The arbitrator will make an award upholding or dismissing the Notice to Quit. An arbitral award upholding the Notice to Quit is not an order for possession. If the tenant does not vacate, then the landlord will have to bring possession proceedings in the County Court.

If the Notice to Quit is referred to arbitration, and the tenant loses, the tenant can nonetheless perhaps still seek to challenge the validity of the Notice to Quit in court, for example by defending possession proceedings on the ground that the Notice to Quit is vague or ambiguous. Whether such rear-guard action is sensible or worthwhile is a matter for the tenant.

Case B: Development

The land is required for use, other than agriculture, for which actual or deemed planning permission has been granted and that fact is stated in the Notice.

Special Case B is very useful because it allows the landlord to recover possession of part of the holding, which is not otherwise possible unless the tenancy agreement so provides. A notice to quit part is invalid under general landlord and tenant law, where the landlord can only recover possession of the whole holding. Case B also allows the landlord to give 'short' notice (i.e., less than the 12 months expiring on a term date which the 1986 Act otherwise requires).

If the Notice is challenged (which is by way of a demand for arbitration: see the discussion of Case A above), it is important that the landlord can prove that she satisfies all the elements of Case B.

There are many reported decisions on the meaning and operation of Case B Notices. Although some general principles can be stated, these are still potentially subject to challenge and argument.

'Required' means that the landlord must have a genuine and firm intention at the date of the notice to develop the notice land, and is not just speculating or land-banking. Except in cases where planning permission is deemed (for example under a General Development Order or an Act of Parliament), planning permission is required. However, the wording of Case B does not require full or detailed planning permission. Outline planning permission may be sufficient, even if it is subject to reserved matters. Although Case B does not contain any time limit, 'required' arguably also carries an element of timing, meaning that the landlord must be able to establish that she is able to implement the planning permission or develop at the date when the Notice expires, or within a reasonable time thereafter. A reasonable time will depend on the circumstances of the case, including the nature of the development. The timing of a Case B Notice to Quit (not too soon, and not too late) can therefore be an issue requiring close thought.

Case C: Bad husbandry

Not more than six months before the notice to quit, the Agricultural Land Tribunal granted a certificate of bad husbandry.

The recovery of possession under this Special Case is begun by the landlord applying to the Tribunal that the Tribunal certify that the tenant is not farming in accordance with the rules of good husbandry. Those are set out in section 11 of the Agriculture Act 1947, and are implied into all 1986 Act tenancies.

Key amongst the rules of good husbandry is the tenant's obligation *'to maintain a reasonable standard of efficient production, as respects both the kind of produce and the quality and quantity thereof, while keeping the unit in a condition to enable such a standard to be maintained in the future...'*.

Before deciding whether to issue a certificate, the Tribunal will visit and inspect the holding and assess its general state and condition. Until fairly recently, there was a widely-held view that Case C was genuinely useful only where agricultural use of the holding, or a significant part of it, had been all but abandoned.

However, some recent cases suggest that the approach of the Tribunal may be changing, with an increased emphasis on the long-term efficiency and economic viability of the holding, leading to certificates of bad husbandry perhaps being easier to obtain than in the past.

A challenge to the grant of such a certificate lies to the Tribunal.

However, if the Tribunal grants a certificate, and the landlord issues a Notice to Quit on the back of it, then the tenant's legal recourse is very limited. If intending to continue to resist possession, then the tenant can either wait for the landlord to issue possession proceedings in court, which the tenant can then defend on the basis that the reason stated cannot be established, or can issue proceedings seeking a declaration that the Notice is invalid. Both these are tactics of last resort, and a tenant would have to reflect carefully as to whether the potential cost of such court proceedings (where, under the Civil Procedure Rules, costs are at large, and may well follow the event) would genuinely justify the steps.

Case D: Rent, and Remediable Breach of covenant

This is divided into two sub-cases.

At the date of the giving of the notice, the tenant has failed to comply with either (a) a Notice to pay rent due or (b) a Notice to remedy a remediable breach.

The recovery of possession by the landlord under Case D is a notice-based system. This means that a successful Case D Notice to Quit is based entirely on the tenant's failure to comply with a relevant earlier notice to pay rent due or notice to remedy a remediable breach. If the tenant has failed to comply with the relevant earlier notice, then the question of whether the rent was ever actually paid, or whether the breach was ever actually remedied, are not relevant.

Given the importance of the notices to pay rent due or remedy a remediable breach, there are very strict requirements as to the wording and service of such notices. Punctilious compliance with the statutory requirements is needed.

Remediable breaches are breaches of covenants which are regarded (as a matter of law) as capable of being remedied. Frequently-encountered examples include breaches of covenants to reside in the farmhouse, or to use the farmhouse as a private dwelling only (this would technically be broken if the tenant used part of the farmhouse as the farm office). Irremediable breaches are dealt with under Case E: see below.

A Notice to Pay Rent or a Notice to Remedy Breach must be in the form prescribed by the Agricultural Holdings (Notices to Pay Rent or Remedy) Regulations 1987 (SI 1987/711). That is a mandatory provision. Hence, a failure to use the correct form will render the whole exercise invalid. The statutory forms are to be found in the Schedule to the Regulations: Form 1 is for rent; Form 2 is for other breaches. There are important 'Act Now' and other statutorily prescribed Notes which must be included.

Compliance with the Notice to Pay Rent is all that really matters. If the tenant pays, but does so after the specified two months, then, although the rent is no longer owed, the tenant has nonetheless failed to comply with the Notice to Pay Rent, and the landlord is entitled to give a Case D Notice to Quit.

It should be clear that tenants who receive notices to pay rent are well-advised to comply with them, immediately, and regardless of any arguments (for example) that the tenant has already paid, or is not liable to pay because convention is that the rent is paid at the annual tenant's dinner, or because the tenant thinks he is entitled to set off rent against a landlord's obligation to him. Non-compliance with a Notice to Pay Rent is a very high-risk strategy since it leaves the tenant with one line of defence against the possession proceedings which will inevitably follow, which is that the notice to pay was not valid on common law grounds (e.g., vagueness).

Challenge to a Case D Notice is by way of a demand for arbitration, in the one-month timescale, followed by an arbitration.

Case E: Remediable Breach

At the date of the notice, the landlord's interest has been materially prejudiced by an irremediable breach of any term or condition of the tenancy agreement, by the tenant, which is not inconsistent with the tenant's duty to farm in accordance with the rules of good husbandry.

Irremediable breaches are breaches of covenants which are regarded – as a matter of law – as incapable of being remedied. These are less common than remediable breaches, which are dealt with under Case D. The most frequently-encountered example of an irremediable breach is an assignment or sub-letting in breach of covenant.

The landlord must be able to demonstrate that the landlord's interest has been *"materially prejudiced"* by the breach. This is undefined, but the breach has got to have a material adverse impact on the reversion. What is 'material' may depend on the circumstances of the case. Moreover, the breach which is alleged to have taken place should be "not inconsistent" with the tenant's duties in respect of good husbandry (see above).

Challenge to a Case E Notice is by way of a demand for arbitration, in the one-month timescale, followed by an arbitration.

Case F: Insolvency

The tenant has become insolvent.

'Insolvent' is defined in section 96(2) of the 1986 Act. For an individual, it means adjudged bankrupt, or entered into an Individual Voluntary Agreement. For a corporate body, it means wound-up or subject to a resolution to wind up. There are obvious gaps in the legislation, which fails to make mention of the Insolvency Act 1986.

This potentially offers a relatively quick and straightforward way of recovering possession. However, the change in the 'bankruptcy limit' (increased in 2015 from £750 to £5000) has inevitably discouraged landlords from issuing a Statutory Demand (which, if not met, could then be used as a springboard to petition for the tenant's bankruptcy) unless they are owed more than £5,000. Of course, rent owing of less than £5,000 – even £1 – is still capable of being the subject of a Notice to Pay Rent which, if not met, will found an incontestable Case D Notice to Quit.

But, if available, Case F is nonetheless very useful to the landlord because the general rule in section 25 that a notice to quit an agricultural holding has to give at least 12 months expiring on the term date does not apply where the tenant is insolvent (s.25(2)(a)), meaning that the landlord can give shorter notice.

Any challenge to a Case F notice has to be in court, either defending the landlord's claim to possession, or bringing a claim for a declaration that the Case F notice is invalid, but bearing in mind the comments above – see Case C – as to the advisability of such a course of action.

Case G: Tenant's death

The tenant has died and less than three months has passed since the landlord received relevant notice.

The tenant's death does not bring the tenancy to an end. It vests in the personal representatives.

'The relevant notice' to the landlord referred to in Case G can be either written notice from the personal representatives (for which there is no prescribed form) or service on the landlord of an application for a succession tenancy (which must be made within three months of the tenant's death).

In the absence of 'relevant notice', time will not begin to run against the landlord for the purposes of the landlord's Case G notice, even if he happens to know of the tenant's death (for example, if he carried the tenant's coffin at the funeral).

In the case of an intestate tenant, written notice has to come from the personal representatives. Therefore, it cannot be given before letters of administration have been obtained.

If the tenant died testate, the personal representatives derive their authority from the will and notification to the landlord at any time after the death by those persons will start time running.

If a succession application is made, then the landlord applies to the Tribunal for consent to the operation of a Case G notice to quit.

Case H: Minister's certificate

Restructuring or reshaping of agricultural units.

This Special Case is only available to the Secretary of State.

CHAPTER FOUR
SUCCESSION TO A 1986 ACT TENANCY

Succession is a very important feature of some tenancies under the 1986 Act. But rights to apply to succeed to an AHT generally exist only where (i) the tenancy was first granted before 12th July 1984, or (ii) if the tenancy was first granted between 12 July 1984 and 1 September 1995, the parties contracted into the succession provisions of the 1986 Act, or (iii) the tenancy itself is a (first) successor tenancy.

Succession rights are potentially exercisable on up to two occasions, on the tenant's death or retirement. The provisions relating to succession on death and on retirement are broadly similar.

Succession applications to the Tribunal on the death of the tenant

The aspirant successor must make an application to the Tribunal within 3 months of the date of death. **Time is of the essence.** This deadline is strict and cannot be extended by the Tribunal. For that reason, it is wise to try to avoid last-minute applications, even if doing so is tempting because (for example) there are discussions between the prospective successor and the landlord. The fact of ongoing discussions, no matter how cordial and productive, does not exempt the applicant from applying to the Tribunal in time. If the applicant does not apply within three months, and negotiations break down, then the applicant is left in real jeopardy.

Use the appropriate Tribunal form (available online) but note that the Tribunal in England and the Tribunal in Wales use different forms. Notice should also be given to the landlord (not least, because the making of an application to succeed starts the landlord's clock running to give a Case G Notice to Quit). The aspirant successor should attach as much supporting information to the form as she can. But the most important thing is to file the application form on time. That should not be put on hold whilst supporting paperwork is assembled. With the Tribunal's permission, that can be provided later.

If the landlord wishes to oppose the application, or comment on it, she must complete and return to the Tribunal the appropriate form within the timescale set down by the Rules.

The landlord can also resist a succession application by issuing a Case G notice, and then applying to the Tribunal for consent to its operation. If this happens, then the Tribunal will first determine the application to succeed before going on to determine whether the landlord's Case G notice should have effect.

An aspirant successor must prove to the Tribunal that she is both 'eligible' and 'suitable'.

Both concepts can present difficulties for applicants. The 1986 Act is now somewhat old, and perhaps showing its age. The legislation was better suited to a model of farms and farming where the farm was economically self-sufficient - in the sense that the farm income was both sufficient to support the farming family (without the need for anyone to work elsewhere) and came entirely from the production of food (and not from activities off the farm, or diversified activities on the farm). These remarks are especially relevant when it comes to consider whether the applicant satisfies the 'livelihood' condition, which is an element of eligibility.

Eligibility

Eligibility is technical, and can be arbitrary.

Close relative

The applicant must be a 'close relative' of the deceased tenant. This is defined by the 1986 Act as meaning a spouse or civil partner, a sibling, a child (including step or adopted children) or "any person (not being a sibling or a child) who, in the case of any marriage or civil partnership to which the deceased was at any time a party, was treated by the deceased as a child of the family in relation to that marriage or civil partnership."

There are obvious omissions from this list, such as grandchildren, nephews, and nieces. They are not 'close relatives', as defined, and therefore are not eligible to apply to succeed and cannot do so. The Tribunal has no power or discretion to consider an application by someone who is not a close relative. If that person wishes to take a tenancy, then they will have to try to negotiate a solution with the landlord.

There are other anomalies. For example, where two siblings (one married with children, one unmarried and childless) hold the tenancy as tenants-in-common, and survivorship operates, whether the children can apply to succeed depends on whether their parent or aunt or uncle dies first.

The 'livelihood condition'

The second part of eligibility is the livelihood condition.

The Applicant must satisfy the Tribunal that '*in the seven years ending with the date of death*' (of the former tenant) the applicant's '*only or principal source of livelihood throughout a continuous period of not less than five years, or two or more discontinuous period together amounting to not less than five years, derived from his agricultural work on the holding or on an agricultural unit of which the holding forms part*': AHA 1986 section 36(3)(a)

This is often the main battleground in disputed applications to succeed to the tenancy.

There are several issues to consider. The first is the proper meaning of 'agricultural work'. Manual work on the farm (milking etc) should straightforwardly qualify. Qualifying work probably includes work which is closely connected with the agricultural activity on the holding, but which is not actually done on the farm, such as agricultural contracting (using the farm's equipment to cut hedges etc for other farmers) or cattle-dealing. It may also catch work which contributes to the agricultural activity but which is 'white collar' rather than muddy boots (for instance, keeping the farm's books and records).

More challenging scenarios can arise where the applicant has worked on the farm, but this work has been part of a diversified enterprise such as running a farm shop, or a B&B in the farmhouse. Such work does not (at least on the face of it) fall squarely within the definition of 'agriculture' given in section 96 of the Act, which has to be met if the tenancy is to be the tenancy of an *agricultural* holding. Whilst some legislative tinkering in 2006 allowed such work to qualify for the purposes of the livelihood condition if the landlord had approved of it in writing, there is no compulsion on a landlord to do so, and it is not obvious why (except for philanthropy) a landlord would want to do so voluntarily.

'Principal' just means 'more than half': 50.01% would be good enough.

'Livelihood' can prove to be a difficult and controversial issue. In the leading case, Casswell v Welby [1995] 71 P & CR 137, the Court of Appeal said that livelihood was to be defined as *'means of living, that is to say what is spent or consumed for the purpose of living. The source of one's livelihood insofar as it is money is income; insofar as it is the use or consumption of goods, it is benefits in kind'*. An applicant may have income derived from one or more sources. If so, in order to qualify, the income derived from work on the agricultural holding must be greater than the income from other sources.

The Court of Appeal was clear that section 36(3)(a) was to be construed in a purposive manner, as a jury would do, and without adopting too legalistic an approach. The section simply requires the Applicant to establish their economic dependence on the holding by showing that their work on the holding provided their main means of livelihood.

Despite this guidance, parties nonetheless do sometimes spend time, effort, and money in a forensic dissection of the applicant's livelihood, in the attempt either (on the part of the applicant) to reach a figure of over 50% (even marginally) for 5 of 7 years, or (on the part of the landlord) to drive the figure down to less (even marginally) than 50% for 3 of 7 years. The Tribunal has itself also, on occasion, been tempted by such efforts, engaging in complex calculations (for example) as to the value of the applicant's bed and board in the farmhouse as opposed to living and eating elsewhere. But parties should reflect on whether such detailed effort reflects the guidance of the Court of Appeal, and whether it is genuinely justified in cases where livelihood, one way or the other, and even on a broad-brush basis, seems fairly clear.

Further complexity is potentially introduced by the issue of resources other than the applicant's. On one view, this is irrelevant: the livelihood test, as set out in the statute, applies only to the applicant for succession, and to no-one else. When it comes to the income of an applicant's spouse or civil partner, it is to be noted that section 36(3)(a) is not an income test, let alone a 'joint income' test. Casswell v Welby itself touches on some of these issues, but it cannot be said for sure that questions as to whether the income or livelihood of an applicant's spouse or civil partner, or the generosity or benevolence of relatives, are always irrelevant.

Here, but only in the event of applications to succeed on the death of the tenant (and not in the event of applications to succeed on the tenant's retirement) section 41 of the 1986 Act provides an important degree of latitude when it comes to assessing the applicant's livelihood. Where an applicant is otherwise, and in all respects, an eligible person, but the source of livelihood test, although not fully satisfied, is satisfied to "a material extent", and it would be fair and reasonable to treat him or her as fully eligible, then the applicant can apply to be treated as fully eligible.

This has to be specifically applied for on the application form. If it is not so applied for, the Tribunal may not be able to consider it. So, and even if you are sure that you will comfortably satisfy the livelihood condition, tick the box!

What is 'a material extent' is a matter of fact and degree. This may depend on whether the failure to meet the livelihood condition was a 'near' miss or not, both in terms of years, and in terms of percentage. As to the latter, the gist of the Tribunal's reported decisions is that something in the region of 40% in any of the seven years which fail to exceed 50% is required. Something significantly less than 40% may fail, on the facts, to satisfy the Tribunal.

The statute gives no further guidance as to what is 'fair and reasonable'. This has to be a matter of fact and degree.

Not an occupier of a commercial unit.

The third element of eligibility, which must be satisfied, is that the applicant must not be in occupation of a commercial unit of agricultural land: section 36(3)(b). The gist of this condition – perhaps reflecting an old-fashioned notion of dynastic farming, with prospective successors staying to work on the farm rather than spreading their wings and going elsewhere – is that a successor has to be economically dependent on their work on *this* holding; and, if they occupy a suitably sized holding elsewhere, capable of supporting them economically, then they will be expected to make their living from that.

A 'commercial unit' is "*a unit of agricultural land which is capable when farmed under competent management of producing a net annual income of an amount not less than the aggregate of the average annual earning of two full-time male agricultural workers, aged 20 or over.*"

There are some complicated rules about this in Schedule 6 of the 1986 Act, and the circumstances in which an applicant is deemed to be in occupation of other land for the purposes of this test.

When an application to succeed to an agricultural tenancy is made, the Tribunals' forms ask the landlord whether the landlord wants a 'Net Annual Income Assessment' to be conducted. This is sometimes referred to as a 'Minister's assessment.' Any Net Annual Income Assessment is performed by the Tribunal (actually, by a specialist appointed and paid for by the Tribunal). It will look at the other land (that is, apart from the holding) which the applicant has declared that she occupies. If the applicant has not declared that they occupy any land other than the holding, then asking for a Net Annual Income Assessment will be pointless, and the Tribunal is unlikely to order one to be conducted, unless the landlord has some decent evidential basis for saying that the applicant is in occupation of other land, but has failed to declare it. If that is the case, the landlord should raise this clearly with the Tribunal. Even then, if an applicant is in occupation of (say) 50 acres of rough upland grazing off the holding, that is unlikely to amount to a commercial unit.

This is because the purpose of the Assessment is to assess any other land occupied by the applicant, so as to establish its 'productive capacity'. The calculation of the productive capacity is done on the basis of the figures set out annually in the Agricultural Holdings (Units of Production) Order. This is a statutory instrument. England and Wales have different orders. The Assessment will produce a figure, and the commercial unit test will be met, or not met.

Suitability

Having dealt with eligibility, the Tribunal must also be satisfied that the applicant is, 'in their opinion', 'a suitable person to become the tenant of the holding'. The suitability test is free-standing from eligibility, and it is certainly possible for an eligible applicant nonetheless not to be suitable to become tenant.

In assessing suitability, section 39(8) of the 1986 Act directs the Tribunal to 'have regard to all relevant matters including (a) the extent to which the applicant has been trained in, or had practical experience of, agriculture; (b) the age, physical health and financial standing of the applicant; and (c) the views (if any) stated by the landlord on the applicant's suitability.

The legal and evidential burden of satisfying the Tribunal is on the Applicant, who must collect and put forward sufficient evidence to satisfy the Tribunal that the Applicant is suitable.

It is to be noted that the statutory factors are not exhaustive. Something sometimes encountered is an applicant who has criminal convictions. These may be potentially relevant (for example, disqualification from driving on the public roads may affect an applicant's ability to get from one part of the holding to another) although the Act is careful to describe the test as one of suitability and not one of moral character.

The Tribunal has a wide discretion. Here, it has to be borne in mind that the Tribunal is usually made up of a panel of three people – a legally qualified chair, sitting with a farmer and a landowner. As such, overly legalistic approaches to the issue of suitability – for example, attempts to require the applicant to demonstrate access to capital reserves as part of their financial standing – may not be the most effective.

There is a general consensus that the Tribunal will overall take a common-sense approach, looking to the statutory factors, and then standing back and asking the general question as to whether the applicant is someone who will pay the rent and keep the farm in good condition.

If an applicant satisfies the Tribunal that she is both eligible and suitable, then (unless the landlord has served a Case G Special Case Notice, and can gain the Tribunal's consent its operation) the Tribunal must make a direction entitling the applicant to the grant of a new tenancy, the terms of which will be the same as the terms of the old tenancy.

Succession applications to the Tribunal on the retirement of the tenant

These are less frequently encountered than applications to succeed on death. Such applications are potentially deterred by two quirks of the rules. The first is that section 41 of the 1986 Act does not apply to applications to succeed on retirement. Therefore, in retirement cases, the applicant has to satisfy the livelihood condition full-stop, and there is no 'material extent' fall-back. The second is that an unsuccessful application for succession on retirement bars the same person from later applying to succeed on the tenant's death.

The rules as to eligibility and suitability are otherwise the same as for applications to succeed on death.

The tenant has to give a retirement notice, and either has to have reached the age of 65 at the date the retirement notice takes effect, or must be permanently physically or mentally incapacitated at that date. The retirement notice has to take effect on the term date at least 12 months from the date of the notice. It must contain the nomination of one person, eligible within the meaning of the Act, as successor. It is not possible to nominate more than one person.

The Resolution of Disputes outside the Tribunal

In relation to FBTs under the 1995 Act, section 28 provides that any dispute between the landlord and tenant under an FBT concerning their rights and obligations under the 1995 Act, 'shall be determined by arbitration'. However, there are exceptions. Section 29 provides that an FBT can contain its own dispute resolution mechanism, therefore overriding section 28.

The 1986 Act provides that many matters of dispute have to be referred to arbitration. Some have been discussed above – for example, Schedule 1 matters, and certain sorts of Special Case Notices to Quit. There are others, such as compensation for fixed equipment, rent review, and settlement of certain claims at the end of the tenancy.

Arbitrations are governed by the Arbitration Act 1996. Section 1 sets out the object of arbitration, which is to obtain the fair resolution of disputes by an impartial tribunal without unnecessary delay or expense, adopting procedures (for example, about evidence, documents, and submissions) which are suitable to the circumstances of the particular case.

Despite these aims, it should not be assumed that arbitration is invariably a quick and straightforward way of resolving the dispute, or even that it will be quicker and more straightforward than going to court.

An important matter to be considered before embarking on arbitration are the potential costs, and the potential incidence of those costs. Arbitrations can be expensive. They are usually conducted by a surveyor appointed by the President of RICS. In contrast to court proceedings, where the judge is paid for through general taxation, the arbitrator will charge the parties a professional fee for their services. Non-lawyer arbitrators sometimes appoint legal advisers or assessors to advise the arbitrator as to legal aspects of the dispute, and this adviser/assessor will also be entitled to charge a professional fee for their services.

The arbitrator may make an award allocating the costs of the arbitration – which are the arbitrator's fees and expenses, the fees and expenses of any arbitral institution concerned, and the legal or other costs of the parties – as between the parties. Unless the parties otherwise agree, the arbitrator shall award costs on the general principle that costs should follow the event except where it appears to the arbitrator that in the circumstances it is not appropriate in relation to the whole or part of the costs: section 61 of the Arbitration Act 1996.

The second aspect is complexity. Except for location and the absence of wigs and gowns, arbitrations can sometimes be indistinguishable from a fully-fledged conventional court case, with witnesses giving oral evidence, and that oral evidence being tested by way of cross-examination.

These factors gave rise to significant and well-publicised criticism of the general operation of the Arbitration Act. In response to this, Schedule 4 of Deregulation Act 2015 now provides that disputes - except in relation to Notices to Quit, which remain the province of the arbitrator, or the Tribunal, as the case may be - can also be resolved by 'third party determination' rather than by arbitration. Third party determination is therefore a possibility, but the rules and governing principles are unclear, and seem to be largely (if not entirely) in the hands of the parties.

CHAPTER FIVE
SUGGESTED FURTHER READING

Halsbury's Laws of England, Volume 1 – 'Agricultural Law and Allotments' (5th edition, 2018, ed. C McNall)

Muir Watt and Moss, 'Agricultural Holdings' (15th edition, 2018, ed Sir T Fancourt and others)

Christopher Rodgers, Agricultural Law (4th edition, 2016)

Scammell Densham and Williams (10th edition, 2015 with supplement, 2018, ed P R Williams) 'The Law of Agricultural Holdings'

MORE BOOKS BY LAW BRIEF PUBLISHING

A selection of our other titles available now:-

'A Practical Guide to the SRA Principles, Individual and Law Firm Codes of Conduct 2019 – What Every Law Firm Needs to Know' by Paul Bennett
'A Practical Guide to Licensing Law for Commercial Property Lawyers' by Niall McCann & Richard Williams
'A Practical Guide to Adoption for Family Lawyers' by Graham Pegg
'Essential Motor Finance Law for the Busy Practitioner' by Richard Humphreys
'A Practical Guide to Industrial Disease Claims' by Andrew Mckie & Ian Skeate
'Employment Law and the Gig Economy' by Nigel Mackay & Annie Powell
'A Practical Guide to the Law of Armed Conflict' by Jo Morris & Libby Anderson
'A Practical Guide to Redundancy' by Philip Hyland
'A Practical Guide to Vicarious Liability' by Mariel Irvine
'A Practical Guide to Claims Arising from Delays in Diagnosing Cancer' by Bella Webb
'A Practical Guide to Applications for Landlord's Consent and Variation of Leases' by Mark Shelton
'A Practical Guide to Relief from Sanctions Post-Mitchell and Denton' by Peter Causton
'Butler's Equine Tax Planning: 2nd Edition' by Julie Butler
'A Practical Guide to Equity Release for Advisors' by Paul Sams
'A Practical Guide to Immigration Law and Tier 1 Entrepreneur Applications' by Sarah Pinder
'A Practical Guide to Unlawful Eviction and Harassment' by Stephanie Lovegrove
'In My Backyard! A Practical Guide to Neighbourhood Plans' by Dr Sue Chadwick
'A Practical Guide to the Law Relating to Food' by Ian Thomas

‘A Practical Guide to the Ending of Assured Shorthold Tenancies’ by Elizabeth Dwomoh
‘Commercial Mediation – A Practical Guide’ by Nick Carr
‘A Practical Guide to Financial Services Claims’ by Chris Hegarty
‘The Law of Houses in Multiple Occupation: A Practical Guide to HMO Proceedings’ by Julian Hunt
‘A Practical Guide to Unlawful Eviction and Harassment’ by Stephanie Lovegrove
‘A Practical Guide to Solicitor and Client Costs’ by Robin Dunne
‘Artificial Intelligence – The Practical Legal Issues’ by John Buyers
‘A Practical Guide to Wrongful Conception, Wrongful Birth and Wrongful Life Claims’ by Rebecca Greenstreet
‘Occupiers, Highways and Defective Premises Claims: A Practical Guide Post-Jackson – 2nd Edition’ by Andrew Mckie
‘A Practical Guide to Financial Ombudsman Service Claims’ by Adam Temple & Robert Scrivenor
‘A Practical Guide to the Law of Enfranchisement and Lease Extension’ by Paul Sams
‘A Practical Guide to Marketing for Lawyers – 2nd Edition’ by Catherine Bailey & Jennet Ingram
'A Practical Guide to Advising Schools on Employment Law' by Jonathan Holden
'Certificates of Lawful Use and Development: A Guide to Making and Determining Applications' by Bob Mc Geady & Meyric Lewis
'A Practical Guide to the Law of Dilapidations' by Mark Shelton
‘A Practical Guide to the 2018 Jackson Personal Injury and Costs Reforms’ by Andrew Mckie
‘A Guide to Consent in Clinical Negligence Post-Montgomery’ by Lauren Sutherland QC
‘A Practical Guide to Running Housing Disrepair and Cavity Wall Claims: 2nd Edition’ by Andrew Mckie & Ian Skeate
‘A Practical Guide to the General Data Protection Regulation (GDPR)’ by Keith Markham
‘A Practical Guide to Digital and Social Media Law for Lawyers’ by Sherree Westell

'A Practical Guide to Holiday Sickness Claims – 2nd Edition' by Andrew Mckie & Ian Skeate
'A Practical Guide to Inheritance Act Claims by Adult Children Post-Ilott v Blue Cross' by Sheila Hamilton Macdonald
'A Practical Guide to Elderly Law' by Justin Patten
'Arguments and Tactics for Personal Injury and Clinical Negligence Claims' by Dorian Williams
'A Practical Guide to QOCS and Fundamental Dishonesty' by James Bentley
'A Practical Guide to Drone Law' by Rufus Ballaster, Andrew Firman, Eleanor Clot
'Practical Mediation: A Guide for Mediators, Advocates, Advisers, Lawyers, and Students in Civil, Commercial, Business, Property, Workplace, and Employment Cases' by Jonathan Dingle with John Sephton
'Practical Horse Law: A Guide for Owners and Riders' by Brenda Gilligan
'A Comparative Guide to Standard Form Construction and Engineering Contracts' by Jon Close
'A Practical Guide to Compliance for Personal Injury Firms Working With Claims Management Companies' by Paul Bennett
'A Practical Guide to the Landlord and Tenant Act 1954: Commercial Tenancies' by Richard Hayes & David Sawtell
'A Practical Guide to Personal Injury Claims Involving Animals' by Jonathan Hand
'A Practical Guide to Psychiatric Claims in Personal Injury' by Liam Ryan
'Introduction to the Law of Community Care in England and Wales' by Alan Robinson
'A Practical Guide to Dog Law for Owners and Others' by Andrea Pitt
'Ellis and Kevan on Credit Hire – 5th Edition' by Aidan Ellis & Tim Kevan
'RTA Allegations of Fraud in a Post-Jackson Era: The Handbook – 2nd Edition' by Andrew Mckie
'RTA Personal Injury Claims: A Practical Guide Post-Jackson' by Andrew Mckie
'On Experts: CPR35 for Lawyers and Experts' by David Boyle
'An Introduction to Personal Injury Law' by David Boyle
'A Practical Guide to Claims Arising From Accidents Abroad and Travel Claims' by Andrew Mckie & Ian Skeate

29526955R10038

Printed in Great Britain
by Amazon